Ala...

by J...

The maps in this book are not to be used for navigation.

Printed in Canada

Coastal Publishing
P.O. Box 110, Vinalhaven, ME 04863

Maps by Joe Upton
Photographs by Joe Upton unless noted with the following abbreviations:
  AMNH - American Museum of Natural History, NY
  AM - Anchorage Museum
  AS - AlaskaStock
  BCARS - British Columbia Archives and Records Service
  BCRM- British Columbia Royal Museum
  CRMM - Columbia River Maritime Museum, Astoria, OR
  DK - Dan Kowalski
  MOHAI - Museum of History and Industry, Seattle
  SFM - San Francisco Maritime Museum
  THS - Tongass Historical Society, Ketchikan, Alaska
  UAF - University of Alaska, Fairbanks
  UW - University of Washington Special Collections
  WAT - Whatcom Cnty (WA) Museum of History and Art

ISBN 978-0-9887981-9-9

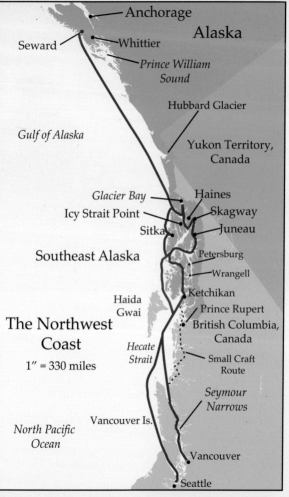

Anchorage

Alaska

Seward

Whittier

Prince William Sound

Hubbard Glacier

Gulf of Alaska

Yukon Territory, Canada

Glacier Bay

Haines

Icy Strait Point

Skagway

Sitka

Juneau

Southeast Alaska

Petersburg

Wrangell

Ketchikan

Haida Gwai

Prince Rupert

The Northwest Coast

British Columbia, Canada

1″ = 330 miles

Hecate Strait

Small Craft Route

Seymour Narrows

Vancouver Is.

North Pacific Ocean

Vancouver

Seattle

This book is primarily about the various major ports along the Inside Passage. But in between lies an intricate maze of waterways. It is the protected nature of these channels and passages, created by immense glaciers carving their way down the coast in the last ice age 30,000 years ago that allows even very small craft to travel the 600 miles between Seattle and the Alaska border.

The Inside Passage is the name for the most common route traveled by smaller craft along the coast. Large cruise ships often adjust their route to stay in wider, less protected waters, when available.

AND A WORD ABOUT THE RAIN

> Visitor to child: "How long has it been raining?"
> Child to visitor: "I don't know. I'm only four."

Let's be frank: it rains here. A lot. My friend Ray Troll, a Ketchikan artist, put it pretty straight:

"Southeast Alaska is the closest you can get to actually living underwater."

That said, it seldom actually pours enough to really stop you from going about your day. It's more like this constant dampness, sort of a permanent misty condition that encourages mold, ferns, drinking, and the temperate rain forest that surrounds pretty much every town, settlement, or remote cabin.

So bring a fleece, a slicker, and enjoy this gorgeous land of ours!

SEATTLE:
THE EMERALD CITY

When Boeing let off more than half of its work force during the recession of 1973, a billboard went up: "Will the last one to leave Seattle turn out the lights?"

Today those days are actually remembered positively. You could park anywhere, drive across town in 15 minutes, buy a great house for $75,000.

Those days are gone, gone, gone... Today Seattle is experiencing painfully rapid growth, whose symptoms are lots of traffic and rapidly rising house prices - median price in popular Capital Hill just topped 1 million.

Yet in spite of this Seattle still retains its unique charm. On the water, with snow capped mountain ranges both to east and west, it is especially popular with lovers of the outdoors.

AND ALSO A GREAT SEAFOOD TOWN

The natives who were here before the whites arrived in the 1840s had a word for the generosity of nature here: "When the tide is out the table is set."

When Seattle character Ivar Haglund opened up a little aquarium on the waterfront in 1938, he noticed that its patrons who plunked down a nickel to view the critters he'd dredged up from nearby Puget Sound brought their appetite as well.

So he started a series of legendary restaurants that still are on any visitors "to eat at" list. Ivar was no slouch either at promotion. One of my favorites was an ad campaign featuring the 'discovery' of underwater ad signs for Ivars, supposedly to lure commuters who traveled by submarine.

Other good seafood restaurants include:

Ray's Boathouse	Cutter's Crabhouse
Anthony's Pier 66	Steelhead Diner
Ivar's Acres of Clams	Duke's Seafood
Chinook's	Taylor Shellfish Oyster Bar
Etta's Seafood	
Pike Place Chowder	Pallisade

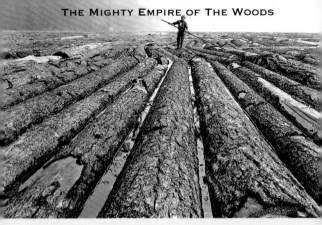

Shortly after Seattle's first settlers built their modest cabin, the sailing ship *Leonesa* arrived, offering a thousand bucks for a load of Douglas Fir for pilings to rebuild earthquake ravaged San Francisco.

The men sharpened their axes, got to work, and the industry that was to dominate the Northwest coast for the rest of the century and

much of the next was born. California and Oregon had lots of good trees too, but didn't have good harbors to load the lumber aboard. Puget Sound had both great stands of Douglas Fir, hemlock, and cedar, and great protected deep-water harbors. Within a few years big mills dotted the shores and ships from all over the world were coming to load.

Photos: UW

As the 21st century opened Puget Sound, especially the east side - the Tacoma to Everett corridor - was booming, led by Boeing, Microsoft, a company that runs coffee shops (Starbucks), and a company that sells everything (Amazon.)

Fortunately the west side, separated by the five or so miles (and even narrower in places) of Puget Sound, retained a much more rural, sleepier quality. Every day the tens of thousands of commuters who crossed the sound every day would drive off the evening ferry to a totally different world than the busy I-5 corridor they had just come from.

   Seattle Art Museum (SAM)- 1300 1st. Ave. Look for tall Hammering Man sculpture. Restaurant, gift shop, many galleries.
*   **Asian Art Museum**
*   **Olympic Sculpture Garden**
*   **Wing Luke Museum**
*   **Museum of Flight**
*   **Chihuly Glass Museum**
*   **Museum of Pop Culture**

*   **Museum of History and Science**
*   **Nordic Heritage Museum**
*   **Burke Museum of Natural History**
*   **Gold Rush Museum**

   Above and left: The Dale Chihuly exhibit at the Seattle Center. If you only have time for one museum, I would recommend this one.

This multi-faceted craft and produce market has been both a vendor of staples for locals, and a strong attraction for visitors. In addition to the market itself and the famous flying fish vendors, the whole neighborhood is full of specialty shops, restaurants - some with a dramatic view of Puget Sound - as well as the original Starbucks coffee shop.

Pioneer Square, straight downhill from Pike Place about 10 blocks, is probably in today's rapidly changing Seattle, the closest you can get to what town used to be like.

It was near here that merchants set up rows of stalls to sell supplies to the many headed North in the Klondike Gold Rush.

Consider taking the Seattle Underground Tour here.

Top: memorial to firemen lost in 1995 warehouse fire.

Right: memorial reads "Chief Seattle, now the streets are our home."

ti
šišəgʷɫ
gʷəl
al tiʔəʔəxʷ
sgʷaʔčɫ
səxʷəsɫaɫlilčəl
siʔaɫ

One of the **Pioneer Square totem poles**, that rotted away years ago, and was replaced by one carved by the same tribe, was originally stolen from an Alaskan village while the inhabitants were out hunting. They were furious when they returned, and chased the robbers' boat by canoe for many miles.

When that one rotted away, the City of Seattle approached the tribe they had stolen it from to carve them another. The tribe responded with a price, but demanded the money up front. When Seattle sent the money, the tribe responded: "That covers the pole that you stole." So they had to pay again before they could get their new pole.

Right: in the Stonington Gallery.

The busiest and most interesting part (from a visitor's standpoint) is the central waterfront extending from the Victoria Clipper ferry dock on the north, 10 blocks or so down to the ferry dock that serves Bainbridge Island and Bremerton. This is also right below Pike Place Market.

In this stretch are the **Seattle Aquarium, a Ferris Wheel** (with enclosed cars), **Ivar's Restaurant,** as well

as numerous other restaurants and shops.

This is also where tens of thousands of gold hungry men bought their supplies and climbed aboard ship to head north in the 1898-9 Klondike Gold Rush.

Left: Gold Rush waterfront. uw

Most folks who come to Seattle for an Alaska cruise just have 24 hours in town or less. Even so, there are some pretty fun activities you can still do:

- **Walk around Fishermen's Terminal**
- **Explore Ballard and the Locks.** Lake Union (which is surrounded by Seattle) and much larger Lake Washington exit to Puget Sound via a set of locks, through which there is much boat traffic.
- **Take excursion vessel** leaving from waterfront.
- **Tillikum Village Native Dance and dinner.** (Ferry leaves from waterfront.)

Take the ferry to Bainbridge Is. (35 min $8 rt), follow the signs to town (15 min.) to eat, explore.

If you have a bit more time, like a few days, and want to explore the Northwest a little further, there are any number of 2-3 day trips that are just spectacular. Here are a few of my favorites:

• **Second Beach and La Push.** Wild ocean coast, ferry + 4 hours. Stay at Quillilute Resort in LP. Do not hike to second beach at high tide (the beach will be gone.)

• **Stehekin.** Remote village at the head of Lake Chelan. Fly or ferry from Chelan, 4 hours from Seattle.

• **North Cascades Highway**. North on I-5, then over Washington Pass, 5 hours, to explore Winthrop area, return via Columbia River or Stevens Pass.

• **Explore Victoria.** The Victoria Clipper round trips daily between Seattle waterfront and Victoria.

Top: Second beach, Left, Stehekin dock.

- **Train to Vancouver.** Amtrak leaves Seattle around 7:30 daily, arrives Vancouver around 11:30. Spectacular ride along the waterfront of Puget Sound and Skagit Valley, and the Fraser River. Plenty to do in Vancouver. Return train every day around 6 for sunset run back with busy club car. Details: Amtrak.com

- **Explore the Columbia River.** Amtrak south to Portland or rent a car for a great loop, along the river to stay in Astoria, then up the Washington coast on US 101, or south along the Oregon coast.

Top: sheep waiting to cross on the old ferry at Klickitat, around 1880. CRMM

*Right: "June Hog" (nickname for very large Columbia River king salmon.*CRMM

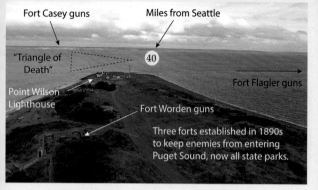

Fort Casey guns

Miles from Seattle

"Triangle of Death"

40

Point Wilson Lighthouse

Fort Flagler guns

Fort Worden guns

Three forts established in 1890s to keep enemies from entering Puget Sound, now all state parks.

MILE 40: THE TRIANGLE OF DEATH

Wanting to protect Puget Sound military installations in the 1920, the Army constructed three forts surrounding the entrance to Puget Sound at Point Wilson, **Mile 40**. The theory was that their intersecting fire would be so intense that no foreign ship could make it through.

Fortunately no one ever tried it, the big cannons were eventually sent elsewhere, and the forts turned into public parks.

The town just south of the Point is Port Townsend, eclectic craft center, particularly well known for its arts community and the care and building of wooden boats.

Left: lapstrake boat outside the Port Townsend Wooden Boat Center.

WOULD YOU GO TO ALASKA IN THIS?

Imagine: all you had to do was to get to the Alaska border in any boat, **but** without using any kind of engine - this was rowing, paddling, sailing, or any combination. And there were 10,000 bucks nailed to a tree, waiting for you! And that's not even the best part. Second prize was a great set of steak knives.

Sounds like something that was put together over beers in a Port Townsend tavern? Pretty much... But the idea became an annual event. A great feature was that each vessel carried an electronic transponder, allowing the position of all the racers to be displayed in real time on the web page. See R2ak.com.

Top: Mad Dog, 2016 winner.
Right: Soggy Beaver, 2015 contender.

VICTORIA

Beginning as a Hudson's Bay Company trading post in 1843, Victoria had a sleepy beginning. But

when gold was discovered in the Fraser Canyon in 1858, Victoria suddenly boomed.

Eventually Vancouver became the industrial and commercial center of British Columbia, and Victoria the capital.

One of the favorite retirement spots for folks from all over the old British Empire, Victoria truly, with its many gardens, feels like Old England.

Left: Bengal Lounge in The Empress Hotel

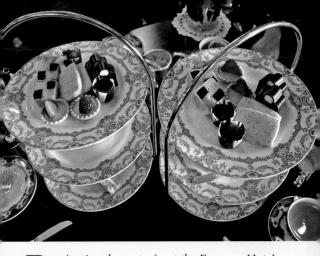

Dominating the waterfront the Empress Hotel - one of many built by the Canadian Pacific Railroad - serves more afternoon high tea than do most hotels in England.

The busy waterfront with the British Columbia Parliament building on the south is the center of activity. Around the harbor are the Wax Museum, the dock for the Port Angeles (USA) ferry, the base for the big float-planes that shuttle over to Vancouver Harbor, restaurants and shops. The wide promenade along the water is particularly popular.

Top: Dessert at high tea at The Empress
Right: Chief Maquinna, leader of the First Nations tribes in the Nootka Sound area of British Columbia in the 1850s.

To the south of The Empress is the **Royal B.C. Museum,** a remarkable institution. With historical dioramas, a National Geographic Imax Theatre, and rotating displays with a heavy emphasis on provincial and First Nations (Native) history, it is highly recommended.

If you don't have time to actually tour the museum, consider at least visiting the lodge house and many restored totems behind the museum, open 24 hrs.

Right: Chilkat (USA) native with Chilkat blanket.

EAGLE-WING-TOURS.com

VICTORIA EXCURSIONS

If your ship gets to Victoria in the morning or early afternoon with a full menu of excursions to choose from, consider yourself lucky, as many southbound ships stop on their way south to Seattle in the evening, limiting the excursions that might be enjoyed.

Victoria Sightseeing Hop On Hop Off Bus
Evening City Tour
A Taste of Victoria
Victoria Castle and City Sightseeing
Butchart Gardens Tour
Deluxe Evening City Tour
Butchart Gardens Illumination
Victoria Whale Watching Tour

If it's the end of your cruise and you haven't seen enough whales, there's a very high chance you can see them here, as there are resident populations of orcas, and usually humpbacks traveling through as well, and the whale tours know right where to go.

There is a shuttle bus from where the big ships tie up to downtown Victoria. But it's also a pretty pleasant 20 minute walk, basically following the water, so consider walking at least one way.

The route passes along some docks where houseboats and yachts are tied up. The seals here are pretty friendly, so if you want to see one up close, this might be a good chance.

Also have a look at the bronze plaques set in the wall overlooking the harbor opposite The Empress Hotel. Many courageous voyages are celebrated here, from the Northwest coast's early explorers to more modern travelers exploring big waters in small craft.

Butchart Gardens is easily the most popular excursion, and for good reason: it's fabulous.

In the 1920s Jeanie Butchart, tired of the mess that was her husband's limestone mining operation, decided to spruce it up with a few flowering plants. One thing just lead to another...

Today it is a 55 acre extravaganza with a restaurant, a multitude of walks, and just exquisite flowers and plants one after another.

For evening visitors in the later part of the summer when dusk comes earlier, there is the illuminated gardens tour. But daylight or dark, don't miss it.

Above photo by M.L Upton

Sailors in the old square rigger days had a name for this coast: The Graveyard of the Pacific." Before

the wonders of electronic navigation, ships would approach the entrance to the Strait of Juan de Fuca often in fog, with no good position fix. The currents would tend to sweep them to the north, toward the dreaded rockbound shore of Vancouver Island.

Top: entrance to La Push, WA. In bad weather, just when you need to get in, it breaks all the way across the entrance.

Above: these guys were lucky; they came ashore on a beach.
MOHAI

P. 28

So many ships wrecked on the southwest shore of Vancouver Island that a shipwreck trail was created, with a path to cabins stocked with food, and a phone to the nearest lighthouse.

Top: outer coast beach. Note the tree, center right. It is about 90' long and 4' in diameter at the base, washed out some river to the ocean and drifted ashore.

Right: buoy with Chinese markings washed ashore near Cape Flattery, WA.

Vancouver is so totally different from Victoria. Cosmopolitan, multi-cultural, industrial, but above all bustling, set on a great harbor with snowy mountains behind and next to the Fraser River, a super highway into the interior, it's a natural for being British Columbia's biggest city.

Like most northwest coastal cities, it started around a sawmill over in what's now North Vancouver around 1863. The next really big event was cross country train service beginning in 1887, that connected with steamships such as the *Empress of Japan* that connected Vancouver with British colonies in Asia.

As the Chinese annexation of Hong Kong approached in 1997, many residents, fearing the unknown, moved to Vancouver along with their substantial wealth.

VANCOUVER

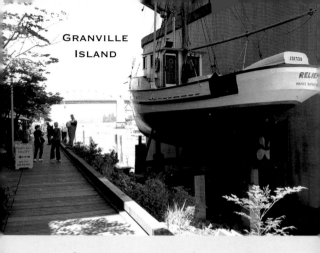

Just south of downtown under the end of the Granville Island Bridge, this area was once an industrial manufacturing area, but today it is now a hot spot for Vancouver tourism and entertainment.

The **Granville Island Public Market** features a farmers' market, day vendors, and artists offering local Vancouver goods. There are 50 permanent retailers and over one-hundred day vendors in stalls throughout the market selling a variety of artisan cottage-industry foods and handmade crafts on a rotating schedule. The popular **Aquabusses** serve the island on a regular schedule.

Vancouver City Tour Including Capilano Suspension Bridge

Vancouver to Victoria and Butchart Gardens Tour by Bus

Whale-Watching Tour from Vancouver

Vancouver City Sightseeing Tour

Summer Tour: Whistler and Shannon Falls All-Day Tour from Vancouver

Vancouver North Shore Day Trip with Capilano Suspension Bridge and ...

Vancouver Harbor Sunset Dinner Cruise

Dr Sun Yat-Sen Chinese Garden Tours

Small-Group Gourmet Food Tour

Grouse Mountain Gondola

And of course, many more...

STANLEY PARK

This thousand acre park deserves a special mention and is one of the key features of Vancouver. Originally the home of several of the First Nations tribes that preceded white settlement, the area evolved into a protected park, including much of the original ancient forest, and now including beaches, a pool, a spectacular set of totem poles as well as miniature golf, the **Vancouver Aquarium**, and an exquisite walk around the seawall.

The great thing is that it is so close to the center of things - a short taxi ride from the **Canada Place**. At the very least have a look at the **Totem Pole Display** and walk around to the view across the channel.

This province markets itself as "Spectacular British Columbia" for a reason: it truly is. Within less than a day's travel is some of the grandest scenery in North America, so plan your trip to include a few extra days to take advantage of it. A few suggestions:

• **Take a Floatplane**: Harbor Air Seaplanes operates right out of Vancouver Harbor to downtown Victoria and many other destinations.

• **B.C. Ferries** operate numerous routes. Just across Georgia Strait from Vancouver are the Canadian Gulf Islands, popular with retirees, boaters, and vacationers. A favorite is Saltspring Island.

Left: kayaker at Skookumchuck Rapids near Egmont, B.C. This is the tide in a narrow passage, not a river or the ocean!

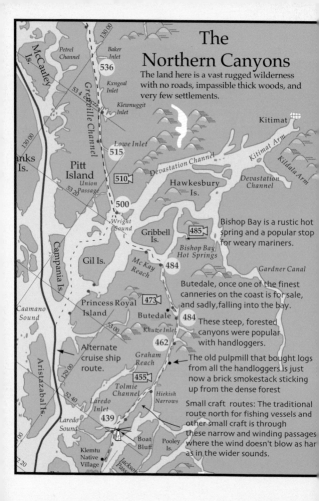

The Northern Canyons

The land here is a vast rugged wilderness with no roads, impassible thick woods, and very few settlements.

McCauley Is.

Petrel Channel

Baker Inlet

536

130.00

Kxngeal Inlet

Klewnuggit Inlet

53.4

Greenville Channel

Lowe Inlet

515

Kitimat

Kitimat Arm

Kitdala Arm

130.00

Banks Is.

Pitt Island

Union Passage

53.2

Devastation Channel

Hawkesbury Is.

Devastation Channel

510

500

Wright Sound

Gribbell Is.

485

Bishop Bay is a rustic hot spring and a popular stop for weary mariners.

Bishop Bay Hot Springs

Gil Is.

McKay Reach

484

Gardner Canal

Campania Is.

Caamano Sound

Princess Royal Island

473

Butedale

484

Butedale, once one of the finest canneries on the coast is for sale, and sadly, falling into the bay.

Khutze Inlet

462

These steep, forested canyons were popular with handloggers.

55.00

Graham Reach

The old pulpmill that bought logs from all the handloggers is now a brick smokestack sticking up from the dense forest

Alternate cruise ship route.

129.00

455

Tolmie Channel

Aristazabal Is.

Laredo Inlet

439

Hiekish Narrows

Small craft routes: The traditional route north for fishing vessels and other small craft is through these narrow and winding passages where the wind doesn't blow as hard as in the wider sounds.

52.40

Laredo Sound

Boat Bluff

Klemtu Native Village

Pooley Is.

22.20

Jackson Passage

The Northern Canyons is my nickname for the northern part of the **traditional Inside Passage** through the mountain heart of British Columbia. Most cruise ships used to take this route, but as they got bigger some of the tighter turns seemed a bit risky, so today most go up wide and boring **Hecate Strait**, spending most of the sea day out of sight of land.

But if your ship does take this much more scenic and exciting route, like the *Volendam* did on this May day (thank you, Captain Turner!) be sure to tell the staff you appreciate it!

Left - numbers are Milemarkers, measured in miles from Seattle. Complete map available on board. The boxed numbers refer to short videos on my website: www.alaskacruisehandbook.com. Above: your author and crew, relaxing after a long Alaska fishing season at **Bishop Bay Hot Springs, Mile 485.**

The big event in Prince Rupert history was when the Grand Trunk Pacific Railroad finally cut its way through the coastal mountains by following the Skeena River and arrived in Prince Rupert in 1914. Farmers throughout Canada wasted no time in exporting their products through "Rupert' (as it is known locally) to Asia.

The railroad transformed the remote townsite into the commercial capital of north coastal British Columbia, with major fish processing plants, wood products plants, and shipping facilities.

For much of the 1900s the nearby **Skeena River salmon runs supported as many as 25 canneries.**

Visitors come to Prince Rupert today to take advantage of its location in the midst of some spectacular scenery and opportunities to see wildlife.

The **Khutzeymateen Grizzly Bear Sanctuary**, for example is about the only place you can reliably see these big boys this side of Kodiak, Alaska. Travelers have also reported being very satisfied with the whale watching excursions. But whatever you do, get outside and enjoy!

- Khutzeymateen Grizzly Bear Sanctuary
- Butze Rapids Park and Trail
- Dolphin & Whale Watching
- Sunken Gardens Park
- North Pacific Cannery Museum
- Museum of Northern British Columbia
- Pacific Mariners Memorial Park
- Port Interpretive Centre (with fast internet)
- Prince Rupert Fire Museum Society
- Breakers Pub
- Maps, etc at **www.princerupert.ca**

Top: guide at the North Pacific Cannery Museum, explains the workings of canning machinery.

Opposite top: Prince Rupert waterfront Tourism Prince Rupert

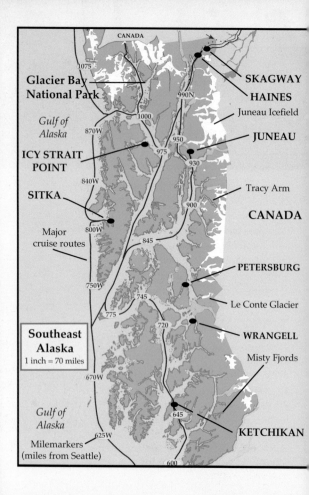

CANADA

1075

Glacier Bay National Park

990N

1000

Gulf of Alaska

870W

950

ICY STRAIT POINT

975

930

840W

SITKA

800W

Juneau Icefield

SKAGWAY

HAINES

JUNEAU

900

Tracy Arm

CANADA

845

Major cruise routes

750W

745

775

720

PETERSBURG

Le Conte Glacier

WRANGELL

Misty Fjords

Southeast Alaska
1 inch = 70 miles

670W

Gulf of Alaska

625W

645

600

KETCHIKAN

Milemarkers (miles from Seattle)

P. 42

About the size of the state of Maine, Southeast Alaska is a vast archipelago of islands large and small, thickly forested and rugged, tucked between the mountain wall of the coastal range to the east and the Gulf of Alaska to the west.

Almost all the land is either National Forest, Monument, or Park. Very little is available for purchase or settlement. At the head of many of the deeper fjords, glaciers calve icebergs.

A few towns are scattered here and there, few connected by road to each other or the outside world.

The big ships stop in the larger towns, often unloading more visitors than the town has inhabitants.

But in the outports, the handful of roadless communities, where fishing is the business at hand, old Alaska lives on.

Two blocks wide and 20 miles long would be a pretty good way to describe this town, scattered along **Tongass Narrows**.

But don't be fooled by today's collection of jewelry shops and t-shirt boutiques in the center of town. This, before the cruise ship industry came and sort of spiffed things up, was a real Alaskan rough and tumble town with a big sawmill right smack in the middle of the dock where the big ships tie up today.

Saturday nights were especially rough when the loggers, fishermen, and mill workers were all looking for a good time. The action centered around the brothels on Creek Street, where as the expression goes, "Men and fish came to spawn."

Above: Asian cannery worker, circa 1920. uw

Ketchikan Pulp, in a big cove north of town was the king of the castle then, offering lots of good paying year round jobs in a fishing town where winter often meant leaner times. In those days fishermen often felt like second class citizens as they tried fruitlessly to stop logging practices that were damaging fish runs.

Then in a stunning move in the mid-1980s, the Forest Service tightened logging regulations and in response, **the mill shut down** (some say it was also having to pay for upgrades to comply with new environmental regulations.) Fortunately the cruise industry was just coming to town with the promise of jobs, though seasonal.

Right: about the only loggers in this part of Alaska are at The Great Alaska Logging Show, downtown.

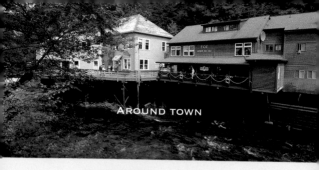

Want to just sniff around a bit without taking an expensive excursion? Some ideas:

- **Explore Creek Street area.** (old red light district) Short walk from the docks, many shops. My Favorite: local fish themed artist Ray Troll's **Soho Coho**.
- **Take the Tram** ($2) Short ride from Creek St. up to Cape Fox lodge with native art, views, & food!
- **Eat like the locals** at the New York Cafe, just south of Creek Street or Annabelle's, 332 Front St.
- **Southeast Alaska Discovery Center** ($5 but National Park Service passes work too). Museum with really good displays on regional history, plus an excellent movie about native culture.
- Explore **Parnassus Books**, next to Creek St.
- **Walk the Docks.** Across the street and just south of Creek Street is Thomas Basin with a wide walkway so you can get a good look at the workboats. Get the **Walking Tour Map** at the Visitor's Bureau on the docks and take the loop up to **Totem Heritage Center.**
- Take the **City Bus to Totem Bight**
- **Walk to Saxman** (2 m., bus goes there too)

KETCHIKAN EXCURSIONS

Misty Fjords - by air or sea, or a combination.
Bering Sea Fishermen's Tour
Coastal Wildlife Cruise
Wilderness Exploration and Crab Feast
Sea Kayaking
Rainforest Wildlife Sanctuary Hike
Neets Bay Bear Watch and Seaplane Flight
Rainforest Ropes Course and Zipline Park
Bear Creek Zipline
Adventure Kart Expedition
Back Country Zodiak Expedition - U Drive
Flightseeing and Crab Feast
Totem Bight Park and Town Tour
Totem Bight and Lumberjack Show Combo
Saxman Native Village tour
Town and Harbor Duck Tour
Motorcycle Tour - U Drive
Sportsfishing Expedition
Sportsfishing & Wilderness Dining (of your catch!)
Alaskan Chef's Table
City Highlights Trolley Tour
Mountain Point Snorkeling Adventure
Note: offerings change frequently

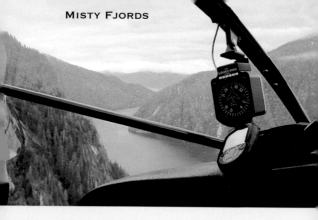

The entire lower southeast corner of Alaska is the vast **Misty Fjords National Monument**. The most popular and scenic part is Smeaton Bay and in particular Punchbowl Cove, overhung with dramatic steep cliffs. Past Punchbowl the channel narrows until it is almost a canyon, opening up to two long arms, popular with kayakers.

Misty is probably the most popular Ketchikan excursion destination. There are several flavors: round-trip by fast catamaran, round-trip by floatplane, which can include a landing inside Misty. Custom flights giving you time to land and fish can also be arranged.

Top: over Misty. Left: in "God's Pocket", nickname for the far inner reaches, past Punchbowl Cove.

CATCHING THOSE BIG ALASKA FISH

Landing a big fish on your Alaska 'to do' list? **Ketchikan and Sitka are probably your best places to try - they're closer to the ocean.**

Most commonly sport fish are silvers, which put up a good fight and run up to 10-12 pounds. Kings are less common and more elusive, but can run to 50 pounds or more. (Record is a 97 pound monster caught on the Soldotna River in 1985.)

Remember that as much as anything else, a fishing trip is a good chance to get out on the water and look for other wildlife such as eagles, otters, and seals.

On occasion eagles have swooped down to steal fish that anglers were hauling in, so watch your line carefully!

Top: silver salmon lures.
Right: Big king and friend. DK

LOOKING FOR BEAR?
Consider asking a taxi-driver - if there have been local sightings, he might know where. It might even be at the dump!

One of the more dramatic of Alaska's many resource booms was the **Bering Sea king crab fishery,** celebrated in the TV series "Deadliest Catch."

Caught in very large pots (6'x6'x2.5') that look more like cages, king crab traveled in large herds along the bottom of the Bering Sea.

In the boom years of the fishery in the 1970s, fishermen loaded their boats quickly and made big, big money. However the weather in the Bering Sea is usually bad to terrible and sadly, many good boats and fishermen were lost in the rough and icy winter fishing conditions.

The *Aleutian Ballad* operates out of Ketchikan, as the **Bering Sea Crab Fishermen's Tour**, giving guests the flavor of this legendary fishery.

Top: my shipmate Walter Kuhr with some big crab, off Unalaska Island, 1971.

Saxman, two miles south along the waterfront from downtown is a good chance to have an up close look at **traditional native culture**.

Modest houses reflect the changing fortunes of making a living from seasonal work. (Much of local income derives from commercial fishing.)

But the totem poles, carving shed, and lodge, where traditional dances are held, show that traditional values are still strong here.

If you're looking for a modest outing this one is for you - just walk south two miles along the waterfront to get there. Regular bus service is also available..

Top: the main lodge at Saxman. Right: carver Nathan Jackson takes a break from his work.

Troller: 35-50', fishes for salmon by towing lures or baited hooks at varying depths behind, targets king and silver salmon. Some freeze fish aboard, others use ice, unload every few days.

Salmon Purse Seiner: limited by law to 58', uses long net to circle fish school, then net is 'pursed' (bottom pulled together to surround fish) crew: 4-5. Works with heavy skiff.

Salmon Gillnetter: 35-45', uses 1800' long by 25' deep net of fine nylon tinted to water color. Often fished by a couple, occasionally with children.

Fish Packers (with gill-netters alongside). Larger, to 100', also called tenders. Buys fish from boats fishing in remote areas. Also supplies water, fuel, groceries, and if you're lucky, a shower.

THE VEGETABLE BOAT

Gone are the days when **the first barge of the season meant fresh vegetables and meat.** (Cattle, pigs, lambs, etc. were brought up alive.) This was especially true on the western rivers where ice stopped navigation for 6 months or more each year.

Today towns in Southeast Alaska get a weekly barge, loaded with vans of food and about anything else that can fit inside.

The big stuff, like the car on the barge above, goes on top. But in the days before the weekly barges, entrepreneurs with fish boats would often load up with groceries in Seattle and head north to a place like Ketchikan, tie up at the town dock and sell right off the boat. Once my friend, Laland Daniels, with his boat, *Christian*, was headed north with a big vegetable load. In rough weather some pumpkins washed overboard, but he made his crew dip them back up before he would head for shelter!

Scattered widely across the islands of Southeast Alaska are the outports, where the big ships never visit and life moves at a very different place. The bigger ones - Tenakee Springs, Elfin Cove, Gustavus, Angoon, and Kake, and, are served occasionally by the Alaska ferries.

But the smaller ones, some with just a handful of residents, like Myers Chuck, Port Alexander, and Baranof Warm Springs, are pretty much on their own, with no road access, and the only way in or out by boat or floatplane. Some are logging camps, but most get by on salmon fishing, sport or commercial, and tourism of some sort. Summers are always busy here, with long days of trying

to make a years' living in a few short months. But then comes the fall, when the outside boats leave for Washington State, and residents settle in for the mellowest part of the year: the long winter.

*Opposite top: homestead at Point Baker, **Mile 742**. Opposite bottom: an overnight catch of bait herring.*

Top: Rosie in her bar/cafe at Tenakee Hot Springs. She remembers the rough days when the cannery was operating and hers was the only place for miles around to get a drink. The cannery closed years ago so it's a lot quieter in this town of a hundred or so folks.

Right: the store at Tenakee is the center of the action.

WRANGELL

When the last logging truck was put on a barge in 2011, Wrangell was just putting the finishing touches on a modest cruise ship facility, in hopes that they could garner some of the benefits that the ships were bringing to the bigger towns.

It's lumber mill had shut down, the local fish processor had gone belly up, and Wrangell was looking for some better economic times.

Seven years later the new economy is clear: modest numbers of cruise ship visitors from the smaller ships. But most importantly, Trident Seafoods took over the defunct Harbor Seafoods Plant, and the town bulldozed and cleaned up the old lumber mill site and bought a large boat hoist to create Wrangell Shipyard.

Consider yourself lucky if your ship stops here; it's the sort of **small town atmosphere** that is gone from the larger towns where a "four ship day" might bring more visitors than the town has inhabitants.

Top: Gillnet fishermen work on their nets in the harbor.

This small town was the busiest spot in Alaska in 1861 and 1873, when the hordes bound for the Stikine and Cassiar gold rushes in British Columbia stopped in Wrangell before they headed up the Stikine River by steamboat, the natural route into interior B.C.

Today the Stikine River is the main attraction for many visitors. On the main migratory route north for many species. April is especially dramatic, when 1500 plus bald eagles congregate to feed on the hooligan (a small oily fish) run, and 8-10,000 snow geese pass through on their way north to nest in the grassy tundra of western Alaska.

Top: Kah Shakes Lodge sits on its own island in the middle of the harbor. The original was built by the Civilian Conservation Corps in 1940, on the site where a much earlier native lodge had stood. It has been recently rebuilt.

THINGS TO DO AROUND TOWN

- **Anan Creek Bear Observatory:** 30 miles south of town, with boardwalks and a viewing stand over a creek where black bears regularly come to catch salmon. Floatplane or boat trips.
- **Le Conte Glacier:** about 45 miles north, is sited in a spectacular bay. Off the big cruise ship route, a flight or a boat trip there might find you totally alone with the big ice, a powerful experience.
- **Stikine River by Jetboat:** The 160 miles between Wrangell and Telegraph Creek in Canada, are especially dramatic, and raft, kayak, floatplane, or jetboats are a great way to explore.
- **Hike the Mt. Dewey Trail:** short well established trail with sections of boardwalk leading up a hill to views over town.
- **Wrangell Museum:** downtown, small, nice.
- **Petrograph Beach:** examples of this native art.

Top: lunchtime at Anan Creek.
Right: Wrangell waterfront: ready for Stikine trips.

CHILDREN SELLING GARNETS?
If you encounter children offering you ruby colored garnets, they're from an old mine on the Stikine, now held in trust for the Children of Wrangell.

When the early Petersburg settlers found **icebergs drifting into the harbor** they thought; "Aha, we can ice our halibut and ship them to Seattle." And so an industry was born.

Settled by Norwegian fishermen who felt right at home with the 10,000' snow-covered peaks right behind town, they got right down to business harvesting the plentiful salmon, shrimp, crab, and halibut.

Today Petersburg and Sitka are the primary fish processing centers of SE Alaska.

The main local processor, Icicle Seafoods, made a major expansion into the fisheries in the Bering Sea in Western Alaska, and then, somewhat to the consternation of the local shareholders, was purchased by a New York based hedge fund, who didn't fully understand what they were getting in to.

Petersburg lies at the north end of **Wrangell Narrows, through which the 20 foot tides rush with considerable velocity.** At the docks and cannery wharves, the current swirls at 4-5 mph, making for some very challenging maneuvering in heavily laden fishboats.

The channel is too shallow and constricted for large ships, but is regularly used by the big Alaska state ferries and innumerable fishing boats and occasional yachts.

Twisting and turning past 60+ buoys and markers, it is particularly challenging in fog or darkness.

Top: tug, towing a log raft winds its way through Wrangell Narrows. Right: navigational light off Petersburg: at high tide the water is almost up to the light on top. Note the dramatic mountains behind.

Visiting nearby LeConte Glacier by floatplane, boat, or kayak is a major attraction for Petersburg visitors. Off the beaten path for the big cruise ships, a visit here would likely find you alone with the big ice, a powerful experience.

LeConte is actually the most southerly place on this

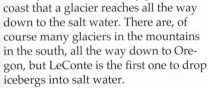

coast that a glacier reaches all the way down to the salt water. There are, of course many glaciers in the mountains in the south, all the way down to Oregon, but LeConte is the first one to drop icebergs into salt water.

The entrance to LeConte is shallow, so you will see bergs stranded by the dropping tide, allowing you to see how much of a berg is underwater: 87%!

Top: photo by Dan Kowalski

THINGS TO DO AROUND TOWN

- **Watch The Waterfront Action:** in summer this is a super busy place with boats coming and going. Can you identify the different boats? (See P. 52)
- **Sing Lee Alley and Sons of Norway Hall:** right downtown next to Fisherman's Memorial and wonderful bronze plaques (one reads :"Ya, ve ha it god in America," commemorating colorful locals.
- **Clausen Memorial Museum:** two blocks up from the water, great place to learn local history.
- **Eagle Roost Park:** walking distance north of town, on the water with great eagle viewing.
- **Whale Watching:** Frederick Sound, north of town is an excellent place to view humpbacks and occasionally orcas. Chances are there also be the occasional small stray iceberg that has wandered out from LeConte Bay!

The core industry of this town is canning salmon. True, these days more and more fish are frozen and shipped off to Japan or China. But by volume, the largest amount of fish landed here are pink salmon, whose most popular product is canned.

When the pinks are running, the whole waterfront is humming with big boats unloading, taking ice, supplies, and heading out again, and the cannery works three shifts: two to can and one for daily clean up and prep.

Salmon roe (eggs) are valuable as well, as a delicacy in Japan. Buyers send staff to oversee sorting and packing and one cannery manager jokingly told me that roe was getting so valuable he was thinking of arming the forklift drivers against holdups!

The first cannery in Alaska was built around 1878. Within a few year the Alaska Packers Association, operating out of San Francisco had purchased numerous old square-rigged sailing ships.

In the early spring these ships would load up with fishermen, carpenters, Chinese cannery workers, boats, nets, canning supplies, and head north.

Arriving at a bay with a strong salmon run, they'd drop anchor. All hands would clear the site, drive pilings along the shore and build a cannery like the one above. Finished just as the salmon were starting to arrive, the gillnet boats would be launched and the fishing and canning would begin.

When the two month season was over, boats would be put away, cans would be loaded aboard, and the ship with all the workers would head south to San Francisco, leaving just a caretaker behind.

And all this without internet, Amazon, or FedEx!

Top: Loring, AK, around 1910 uw

JUNEAU:
ALASKA'S UNLIKELY CAPITAL

Like Skagway, it was gold that brought Juneau's first white settlers. However, the easy to find streambed gold was quickly gathered up, and a new kind of enterprise was formed to follow the gold underground. This industrial scale deep tunnel hard rock mining was very different from other Alaska gold rushes where individuals or small groups of men worked creeks and beaches with essentially hand tools.

At Juneau, high grade ore was quickly exhausted and massive stamp mills were built to extract gold; it wasn't uncommon for 20 or more tons of ore to be dug and processed to yield a single ounce of fine gold. The tailings - the crushed rock that was left, were dumped along the shore to create the land on which much of downtown Juneau was built on.

Left: tram pulls into upper station. Above: the big stamp mills of the Alaska Juneau mine, around 1905. Today this is the main berthing area for cruise ships.

Deeper and deeper they dug at the Treadwell Mine, creating great rooms, held up by posts of the same ore, deep under Gastineau Channel.

Then when the gold content dropped, they went

back and started removing posts, shaving others, to get at that high gold content ore.

As if to warn them, the mine groaned, cracked, and finally collapsed and filled with salt water.

Today it's government, state and Federal, that are the steady employers here in a town where moose sightings are not uncommon and the only way in or out is by ferry or airplane.

Traces of the mining days are scattered in the hills behind town: tumble down barns for mining locomotives, rusting mine cars, miles and miles of tracks.

And from the numerous old entrances cool breezes blow, giving a sense of the size of the maze of tunnels, which still are explored by adventuresome Juneauites.

Opposite page top: old train barn near the Last Chance Mining Museum.

Top: one of the largest air compressors ever built is on display in the mining museum in Silver Bow Basin behind town.

The **A J Mine Gastineau Mill Tour** gives a thorough overview of the mining process.

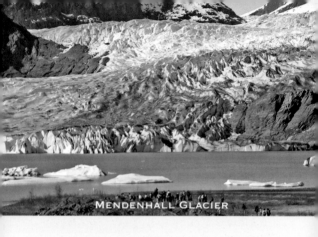

MENDENHALL GLACIER

About the size of Rhode Island, the Juneau Ice Field stretches for miles up and behind Juneau. One of its glacier tongues is Mendenhall, disgorging small bergs into a lake.

It is also a **very rapidly receding glacier:** compare the above to the 1956 photo below where the ice is almost at the hill the viewers are standing on above.

There's a lot of ways to see Mendenhall; many excursions include it. The Bus ($20 rt) is the cheapest and easiest, but there are also:

-Mendenhall Glacier Canoe Paddle and Trek

-Mendenhall Glacier and River Rafting.

-Mendenhall Hike (with crampons up onto the glacier.)

JUNEAU WHALE WATCHING

Lower Lynn Canal close to Juneau to the west has a **healthy summer population of both hump-back and orca whales**. If you haven't seen whales up close yet, and Sitka (another good place to whale watch) isn't on your itinerary, consider an excursion here. Most of the tours also include a stop at Mendenhall Glacier as well.

Humpbacks, running up to around 50' long are the most common whale seen in this part of Alaska.  Straining small fish through sieve-like baleen in their jaws, they will fatten up here over the summer before they head to Hawaii for the winter.

Orcas are smaller, to 20', and are recognized by their dramatic black and white markings, and a very tall dorsal fin. Orcas or killer whales, are aggressive eaters of salmon, sea lions, seals, and small whales.

Around town

- **Stairways** - how'd you like to carry your groceries up these stairs in winter? A lot of folks do.
- **Take the Flume Trail** - off the road to the Last Chance Basin, connects with upper downtown.
- **Visit the Native Museum** -105 S. Seward St. Small but exquisitely done with good gift shop.

- Eat at **The Hangar Bar** or **Alaska Fish & Chips**. Both offer a great view of the floatplanes coming and going. Another good seafood spot is **Twisted Fish,** south of the Tram. Crab? Hit **Tracy's King Crab shack.**
- **Quiet Free Wi-fi** even with a view. Juneau Library by dock.
- **Mt. Juneau Trading Post** - 151 S. Franklin St. Owned by Native family, almost a museum!

Mendenhall Glacier (in many flavors, kayak, etc.)
Original Alaska Salmon Bake
Rainforest Garden
A Taste Of Juneau
Dog Sled Summer Camp
Gold Panning & History Tour
Glacier View Bike & Brew
Rainforest Canopy & Zipline Expedition
Juneau Sportfishing Adventure
Juneau Steamboat Cruise
Photo Safari By Land & Sea
Whale Watching & Wildlife Quest
Taku Glacier Lodge Flight & Feast
Pilot's Choice Ice Age Exploration
Mendenhall Glacier Helicopter Tour
Four Glacier Adventure By Helicopter
Glacier & Dog Sled Adventure By Helicopter
Dog Sledding On The Mendenhall
Note: Not a complete list, changes often!

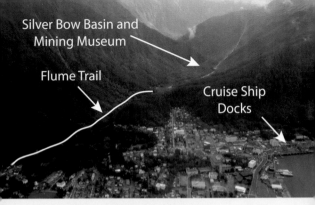

Silver Bow Basin and Mining Museum

Flume Trail

Cruise Ship Docks

HIKE THE FLUME

Part of Juneau's water system, the flume is a **long wooden aqueduct** from the Silver Bow Basin to downtown. But smart town fathers built a **walkway on top**! Be careful: parts can be slippery!

Getting there: walk up Franklin St. uphill to 7 th.

Turn right, go one block to Gold, turn left, follow up and around, turn left on Basin Rd. and walk about 1/4 mile to Flume trail entrance on left.

At end of flume: follow street to the "to the Stairs" sign on left, carefully (!) down steep stairs, down and left at cemetery, and back downtown, passing Governor's Mansion with totem pole on right. There's a **street map available at visitor's center** on the cruise ship docks by the tram.

TRAM TIPS

- **Go as late as you can** (light for photos is better).
- **Hike the upper trails** (carefully..) for better views.
- **Eat with a view** - great seafood in the restaurant.
- **Wear good footwear**, esp. on the upper trails.
- **Consider ride up/hike down** or vice versa, but be aware the trail down can be slippery and rooty..

Alaska.

SKAGWAY
AND
THE GHOSTS OF '98

The hard-faced men, bent over with their packs, that came to town on their way to the long struggle that was the **1897-98 Gold Rush**, have passed on, but Skagway sometimes seems filled with their ghosts.

In a wet maritime climate like Ketchikan, these buildings would have rotted long ago, but in Skagway's much drier interior climate, they stand today, monuments to the drama that so briefly filled the town.

After the Gold Rush was over, the town shrunk to less than a thousand, subsisting on income from the railroad transporting ore. But finally even that dried up and the railroad closed and town got even quieter.

Then the big ships started coming, the railroad re-invented itself and town became what you see today.

Left: look at these faces: Yukon prospectors, 1897 uw

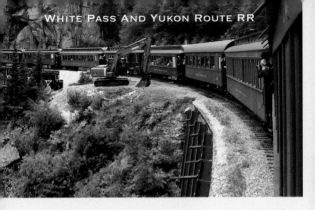

In 1972 the old stream engines were at the end of the track, ready to be pushed into the water or sold for scrap metal.

Then came the cruise ship boom and the tiny town of Skagway and its core population of 1,000 exploded each year for a few short months of as many as 10,000 visitors a day.

The best remaining steam engine, old 73, was rebuilt and put back on the run. (In 2018, it is being rebuilt yet again, to be back in service in 2019.)

Classic rail cars were purchased and refitted to create what is now the most popular excursion in Alaska.

Available in several schedules and routes. See opposite page.

Left: front end of big steam powered rotary snowplow.

ALL ABOARD!

Note: passengers making excursion reservations aboard ship, will board the train near the ship. Others board downtown. Reservations required.

Train Schedule
Skagway to White Pass RT
8:15 AM & 12:45 PM DAILY
4:30 PM Tu.& Wed. ONLY
$125 adult, $62.50 child

Lake Bennett Scenic Journey
Train up, bus return:
7:45 AM: Tu., Wed., Th., Fr. & Sat.
Bus up, train return:
9:30 AM: Tu., Wed, Th., Sat. & Sun.
$234 adult, $62.50 child
Other options, details:
www.wpyr.com

CORRINGTON'S IVORY MUSEUM

When Dennis Corrington was a schoolteacher, he got to know many of his native students' families and became interested in marketing their ivory carvings.

He next commissioned pieces of walrus tusk ivory to celebrate the history of Alaska.

Moving to Skagway, he put his collection, and much more, into a free museum in his gift gallery.

Don't miss it!

SKAGWAY EXCURSIONS

Skagway & The Dangerous Days Of '98
Klondike Summit & Liarsville Experience
Klondike Summit, Bridge, & Salmon Bake
Historical Tour & Liarsville Salmon Bake
Skagway's Original Street Car
Experience The Yukon
White Pass Scenic Railway
Best Of Skagway
Klondike Scenic Highlights
Delectable Jewell Gardens
Deluxe Klondike Rail Adventure
Alaska Garden & Gourmet Tour
Yukon Jeep Adventure
Horseback Riding Adventure
Klondike Bicycle Tour
Klondike Rock Climbing & Rappelling
Alaska Sled Dog & Musher's Camp
Chilkoot Trail Hike & Float Adventure
Glacier Point Wilderness Safari
Glacier Lake Kayak & Scenic Railway
Dog Sledding & Glacier Flightseeing
Glacier Discovery By Helicopter
Heli-Hike & Rail Adventure
Alaska Nature & Wildlife Expedition
Remote Coastal Nature Hike
Takshanuk Mountain Trail By 4x4
Eagle Preserve Wildlife River Adventure
Chilkoot Lake Freshwater Fishing
Wilderness Kayak Experience
Skagway's Custom Classic Cars
Glacier Country Flightseeing
Note: Incomplete list: check on ship or in port.

AROUND TOWN

- **Bites on Broadway:** 648 Broadway - great pastries, sandwiches, coffee, opens early, even a B & B!
- **Skagway Fish Co:** on the dock; excellent.
- **Red Onion Saloon:** if only the walls could talk!
- **Bonanza Bar & Grill:** rowdy, good pub food.
- **Rent a Bike:** Sockeye Cycle, 381 5th st.
- **Free Wi-Fi & Quiet:** Library, 8th & State St.
- **Hike to Dewey Lake:** short, steep, climb to pleasant walks around lake.
- **Hike out to the Gold Rush Cemetery**
- **Hike Chilkoot Pass.** Difficult, multi-day.

Note: there are more restaurants than just these.

Top: Nils and Skipper, owners and operators of Bites on Broadway.

Up at the head of Taiya Inlet, Dyea, like Skagway was the jumping off place for the thousands of men and a handful of women headed to the Yukon in the fall of 1897.

When it was built, it was on the water, but after the immense weight of the glaciers that covered all this part of Alaska receded, the ground rose at the rate of about 3/4" per year or over 6' since the Gold Rush, pushing the high tide almost a quarter mile further away on this sloping shore.

With no railroad to sustain it **after the Gold Rush Dyea eventually disappeared.**

Today hikers headed to Chilkoot Pass, nicknamed a "33 mile museum" pass through what's left.

Right: Klondikers come ashore at Dyea. UW

One of the saddest part of the Gold Rush was the number of graves simply marked 'Unknown.' Some men came north leaving families behind, families who waited and waited but never got word. Communication was poor, not everyone had any i.d. People just disappeared.

UNKNOWN

The father of one farm family from Eastern Washington headed north with the thousands of others in the fall of 1897. Two years passed without a word. Running out of money and with two children, his wife was frantic. Finally she went to Seattle, to stand at the gangway of an Alaska ship, to ask for any word of her husband.

And down he stepped, carrying a heavy suitcase with his gold!

Helicopter excursions in Juneau and Skagway can give you a sense of the drama and beauty of the vast wilderness of ice and rock in the nearby mountains. These are pricey ($300-$350) excursions, but getting up onto the ice, walking around seeing the crevasses up close, etc. is a fascinating experience.

Another option is flying to a camp on the glacier where there are sled dogs waiting eagerly, barking as soon as they see an inbound chopper as they know they're about to do their favorite thing: pull, pull, pull. These are more expensive ($500 or more) but folks who have gone report being thrilled!

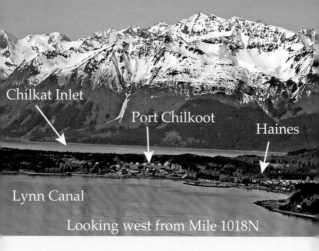

Glacier Bay lies beyond these mountains.

Chilkat Inlet

Port Chilkoot

Haines

Lynn Canal

Looking west from Mile 1018N

Just 20 miles south and a world away from super-busy Skagway are these side by side communities - totally small town Alaska.

Port Chilkoot used to be an Army base; now the buildings are residences, studios, and small businesses, including a smokehouse and a distillery.

Haines settled into a quieter existence after the sawmill closed in 1991, and bills itself as "The Adventure Capital of Alaska."

Its biggest draw is the **Southeast Alaska State Fair** each summer and the **Bald Eagle Festival** each November as thousands of these big birds gather to chow down on the thousands of dog or chum salmon that have spawned and died.

It's a great place to see wildlife on **boat tours up the Chilkat River**

HAINES AND PORT CHILKOOT

- **Visit The Hammer Museum:**
- **Raft or cruise The Chilkat River**
- **Visit the Sheldon Museum**
- **Great Alaska Craft Beer and Home Brew Festival:** (Memorial Day weekend)
- **Bald Eagle Festival** (second week of November)
- **Rent a Bike** at Sockeye Cycle or Mike's Cycle

We are Not like Skagway

We get very few ship dockings
We are self-owned shops
We are not owned by the cruise lines

Please help support Haines!

The braided channels of the Chilkat River offer a perfect spawning ground for hundreds of thousands of dog or chum salmon each fall. These salmon die after spawning, and some 1500 eagles arrive here each fall for a feast that lasts for weeks. It is the largest assemblage of eagles in North America.

SALMON BOOM DAYS
IN CHILKAT INLET.

In the early 1970s the booming Japanese market for all things salmon coincided with some very **strong dog or chum salmon runs in the Chilkat River.** **Several hundred gillnet vessels** from all over Southeast Alaska would gather here in September to try and double their season in a few short weeks.

In order to control the harvest with so many boats,

fishing was limited to only one day a week! However, **at $1 a pound, many boats could catch 8 or 10,000 pounds a week**, making it well worth it.

The other challenge was the weather: Lynn Canal was a notorious wind tunnel, and as you can see from the above photo taken on Oct. 4, snow came early!

P. 90

BUILDING A ROAD HERE:
IS IT EVEN POSSIBLE?

If you see a "Build The Road" or "Stop The Road" bumper sticker, the road in question is the proposed one from Juneau to a (presently non-existent) ferry dock near the above location just across Lynn Canal from Haines.

The rationale is that such a road would give Juneau residents a road to the "outside," and provide better health care services (in Juneau) for Skagway and Haines residents.

However, most of the route the road would have to be built on is similar to the above, with many avalanche chutes that might be difficut to keep open in a hard winter.

Plus, the road wouldn't even get all the way to Skagway as the terrain is almost vertical rock walls rising up from the water the last miles into town.

EXPLORING PORT CHILKOOT,
THE ARTS CENTER OF HAINES

- Seawolf Gallery:
- Alaska Indian Arts Center
- Port Chilkoot Distillery
- Wild Iris Gallery

- **Dejon Delights Smoked Salmon Shop**
- **Wayne Price Studio:** master Tlingit carver and canoe maker.
- **Fireweed Restaurant**
- **Pilot Light Restaurant**
- **Ferry to Skagway:** 45 min., multiple sailings daily, $72 adult round trip.

Port Chilkoot, originally Fort Seward was the **first permanent army fort** built in Alaska in 1904 as a peacekeeping fort - keeping the peace between settlers, miners, Natives, and cannery workers, as well as with the Canadians. The fort was **purchased in 1947 by a group of World War II veterans whose vision was to make an arts center in Alaska.** To a great extent they succeeded as they were instrumental in reviving Native art and totem carving and creating a visitor attraction. For more: **www.VisitHaines.com**

> **If You Lived Here, I'd Know Your Name**
> by Haines author Heather Lende is a fine read on Alaska small town life.

When the **old Hoonah Packing Company cannery** stopped processing fish in 1953, it seemed destined to be used for a few years as a storage facility for fishermen's gear and eventually abandoned, to become just ruins and pilings on the beach, like many old canneries.

But instead the Hoonah Native tribe realized the old cannery might be a way to showcase the salmon industry, Native culture, and create some jobs and revenue for the tribe as well.

What you see there today is **unique among all Alaska cruise ports: a privately owned cruise port, allowing just one ship at a time,** creating a very different visitor experience than in any other Alaska port.

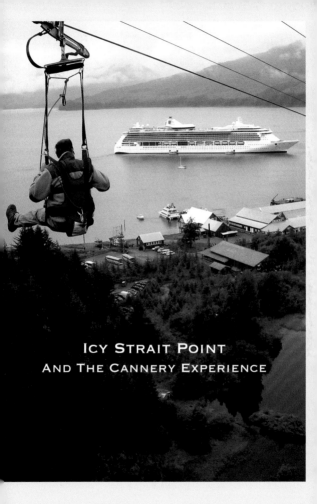

ICY STRAIT POINT
AND THE CANNERY EXPERIENCE

Catching and canning salmon was the core indus-try in SE Alaska for generations. From the 1880s when Asian workers used tin snips and solder to make the cans out of sheets of tin, to today's mechanized production lines the process is essentially the same: clean and cut the fish to fit into the can, and cook the cans with the lid on in big pressure cookers.

Top: workers with retorts diorama at Icy Strait Point. The retort is essentially a big pressure cooker with doors at both ends and a track through the middle to hold 'cars' containing racks of cans. Left: worker readying cans for filling.

In small cannery based towns like Hoonah, life revolved around salmon fishing and processing. Spring was a time for getting the boats, nets, cannery, and processing equipment ready.

Then on schedule like they had been before even the natives made their way across the Bering Land Bridge to Alaska, the salmon began arriving, and the frenzy of 'the run' began. In a big year the cannery worked around the clock, and men and boats struggled to make a year's pay in three or four short months. Winter was time to sit back. And think about the season to come!

- **Whale Watching**
- **Wildlife Tour**
- **Zip lining**
- **Hoonah Scenic Drive**
- **Tribal Dance Show**

- **Culinary Tour**
- **Kayaking**
- **ATV Expedition**
- **Sport Fishing**
- **Bike Tour**

Note: excursions change frequently, check aboard.

Take the shuttle or hike the mile and half to town and you'll see right away why the early settlers picked this place. With plenty of flat land behind a long south facing beach, it was perfect for a people that depended on the sea for their livelihood. The modest homes reflect the ups and downs of a resource-based income - much of the tribe depends on income from fishing and logging.

Top: Hoonah Cold Storage dock. The cannery stopped long ago, but fishermen are still able to land halibut, salmon, black cod, and crab catches here to be frozen and shipped to Seattle or Asia. The boats at the dock with the tall poles are salmon trollers.

Right: Nature walk on smooth groomed trails behind the cannery.

WalkaboutHoonah phone app available.

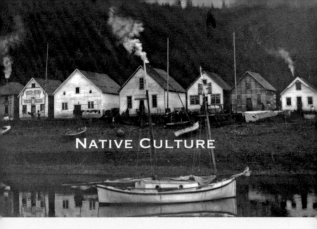

I t's generally accepted that during the last ice age, around 30,000 years ago, so much of the Earth's water was frozen into glaciers that the sea levels dropped enough in the Bering Strait area to create dry land between what is now Siberia and Alaska. And that hunters and their families, probably chasing game, walked across, becoming the tribes that eventually settled much of North America.

In SE Alaska they found a mild climate and abundant seafood, allowing them to create permanent village sites, so much so that they were known to the interior tribes, who had to move from place to place in search of game, as "People who live in big houses."

The Hoonahs originally lived

across Icy Strait along the southern shores of Glacier Bay. But when the ice pushed south in the middle 1700s, they moved across the Strait, naming their present home Hoonah, which in Tlingit means "Where the North Wind Doesn't Blow."

However they continued to hunt seals in the Glacier Bay area, and actually provided a guide for John Muir's explorations of the great bay beginning in 1867.

Top left: Hoonah, around 1900.

Lower left: grave marker in Hoonah cemetery.

Top: Tlingit natives in Sitka area, circa 1870.

Right: Tlingits in ceremonial regalia. Photos: Isabel Miller Museum, Sitka.

Sitka was the capital when Alaska was part of Russia from the late 1700s until 1867, an empire based on sea otter fur, the Russians sometimes slaughtering whole native villages if they didn't kill enough otters.

Those were good years when Sitka was the busiest

port on the Northwest Coast. Its residents drank fine wines and enjoyed ballet, at a time when Ketchikan and Juneau were native villages.

After the Russians slaughtered the sea otters almost to extinction, and lost the Crimean war in the 1850s, they were almost broke, and sold Alaska to the U.S. It was a great deal for the US: $7.2 million, about 2 cents an acre, and was completed in 1867.

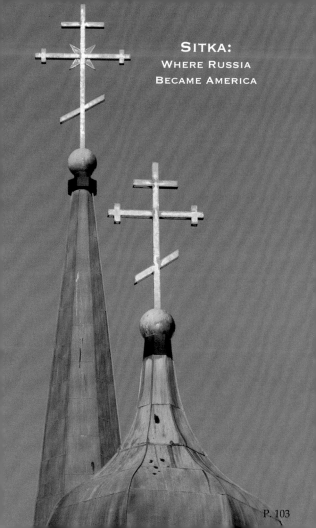

SITKA:
WHERE RUSSIA
BECAME AMERICA

In modern times the busy plywood mill out in Sawmill Cove provided a strong base of steady good paying year round jobs. The closure of the mill in 1992 was a big financial blow, but in the years since the town has experienced a slow renaissance based on the arts, commercial fishing, and, to a lesser degree, tourism.

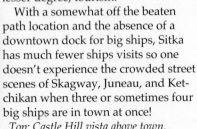

With a somewhat off the beaten path location and the absence of a downtown dock for big ships, Sitka has much fewer ships visits so one doesn't experience the crowded street scenes of Skagway, Juneau, and Ketchikan when three or sometimes four big ships are in town at once!

Top: Castle Hill vista above town.

Russian America History Tour
Russian America & Raptor Center Tour
Sitka Nature & History Walk
Sitka Bike & Hike Tour
Advanced Bike Adventure
Tongass Rainforest Hike
4x4 Wilderness Adventure
Sitka Sportfishing
Wilderness Sea Kayaking
Dry Suit Snorkel Adventure
Sea Life Discovery Submersible
Sea Otter & Wildlife Quest
Sea Otter Quest & Raptor Center
Silver Bay Cruise & Hatchery Tour
Wildlife Quest & Beach Trek
Change often; check on board.

Top: snowy owl at Raptor Center.

Rent a Kayak
If you just want to go off on your own &
there's plenty to explore: **kayaksitka.com**

With a close to the ocean location, Sitka is a much better place for sportsfishing than Juneau or Skagway. Also the high speed catamaran excursion boats, built locally, allow access to excellent whale watching and scenic island vistas.

And plenty else, just a sample:

- **Archangel Dancers**
- **Ludvig's Bistro**: small, intimate.
- **Paradise Cafe**: waterfront.
- **Backdoor Cafe:** in bookstore!
- **St. Michael Cathedral**
- **Bishop's House**: built in 1842.
- **Castle Hill**: great views!
- **Sheldon Jackson Museum**
- **Alaska Raptor Center**: big birds up close and personal!
- **Quiet free internet**: public library, 320 Harbor Drive.

Top: inside St. Michael's Cathedral.

There's a **really pleasant walk** that starts by Crescent Harbor just east of downtown. Continue east along the waterfront, past the sign about salmon habitat and eventually into the grounds of the **Sitka National Historical Park** - hint: totem poles in front.

Inside the main building are an active carver, historical displays, gift shop, etc. Continuing onto the grounds, there are trails with totem poles here and there in the woods and a nice stream with salmon sometimes visible in July and August. Take the trail out of the park, cross Halibut Point Rd. turn left, walk about a hundred yards and go up the driveway on the right to the **Alaska Raptor Center.**

On the way back; **Sheldon Jackson Museum**. *Top photo: Isabel Miller Museum, Sitka*

SHELDON JACKSON MUSEUM

Sheldon Jackson (1834-1909), a Presbyterian minister and missionary found his life's work in Alaska helping the natives, particularly the Yup'ik and Inupiat (eskimo) tribes of Western Alaska. He was instrumental in importing 1,300 reindeer from Siberia, which became an important food source.

Some of the best of the items he collected from Western Alaska are here in the museum named for him.

Top: Eskimo mannequin dressed in rain gear made from strips of seal or walrus intestines. Left: sweat lodge model.

THE APRIL FOOL'S VOLCANO

Mt. Edgecumbe is the dramatic 3,201' volcano that looms over Sitka. It has been dormant for some 4,000 years but **on April 1, 1974, word quickly flashed around town that she was gonna' blow, as dark smoke was billowing up from the crater.**

Aircraft were quickly scrambled to fly around the crater to try and determine if a major eruption was beginning that could possibly threaten Sitka with ash or worse.

But as soon as they got close the pilots realized the whole town had been had: the smoke was from a pile of old tires and "APRIL'S FOOL" was painted in 50' high letters in the snow!

Most passengers end or begin their cruise at these towns and spend little time. Whittier, a tiny ex- army base, where everyone used to live in one big building that housed barber, theatre, etc. is accessed by a 2.5 mile tunnel under the mountains, and has a few modest shops and restaurants around the waterfront. **Tip: if you have a choice of train or bus to/from Anchorage, choose the train.**

Seward is much more substantial with numerous attractions including the **Alaska Sealife Center,** its many murals, **Exit Glacier,** that you can walk up to (after you drive there), a very active sports and commercial fishing scene, and the headquarters for the **Kenai Fjords National Park**, with its actively calving glaciers.

Right: excursion in Chiswell Islands, Kenai Fjords N.P.

Traveling Northwest waters as a commercial fisherman for 20 years, Joe Upton gained intimate knowledge of the coast from Puget Sound to the Bering Sea.

In the 1970s Upton lived and fished out of a tiny island community in the roadless wilderness of Southeast Alaska. His first book, *Alaska Blues*, based on those years, was an instant classic.

In 1995 Upton established Coastal Publishing to share with the new travelers to Alaska some of the drama he had seen in his travels, producing illustrated maps and *The Alaska Cruise Handbook*.

In 2010 Upton teamed up with filmmaker Dan Kowalski to produce mini-documentary films that can be accessed at **www.alaskacruisehandbook.com**.

Upton lives with his wife on Bainbridge Island, WA, and Vinalhaven Island, ME.